The Wonder of Travel

By Sally Cowan

Contents

Come Travelling!

When you go from one place to another, you travel.

You can travel somewhere close to home, or you can cover a long distance.

Close to Home

Ava loves school!
She travels to school in her mother's van.

In a few months, Ava will turn eight.
Then she will catch the bus with her brother.

Some children travel to school on bikes.

These kids put on helmets and sometimes gloves, too.

Travel with Animals

Today, we are lucky to have bikes and buses.

Long ago, people had nothing but animals and wagons.
It could take months to get somewhere.

Some people still travel around with animals.

These kids ride in a wagon pulled by animals.
It's a nice way to go to school.
They chat with one another on the ride.

These men ride camels across sand dunes.

Camels are the best way to travel in the desert.
They can cover long distances with very little water.

Planes and Ships

To cover a long distance, we can take a plane or a ship.

But it can cost lots of money to travel far away.

Caleb is lucky.
He will travel by plane to visit his aunt and uncle in another city.

He will fly above the clouds!

We can travel across the sea on a cruise ship.

Some people love to go on cruises for months!
They visit dozens of places.

A ship is slower than a plane, but there is a lot to do and see on a cruise ship.

A whale might even come close to the ship.
Wonderful!

Travel to Other Planets

One day, we might have the chance to travel to **very** distant places, like Venus or other planets!

It would be amazing to see Earth from above.

Earth

I would love to travel to Saturn.

I wonder how long it would take!

CHECKING FOR MEANING

1. What are three ways to travel? *(Literal)*
2. What might you see from a cruise ship if it comes close? *(Literal)*
3. Why do the kids on page 4 put on helmets? *(Inferential)*
4. What do you think is the best way to travel? Why? *(Evaluative)*

EXTENDING VOCABULARY

desert	What kind of place is a desert? How is a desert different from the beach? How is it the same?
dozens	How many things are in a dozen? What sorts of things can you buy in dozens?
wonder	What does the word *wonder* mean in the text? What are you doing if you are wondering about something?

MOVING BEYOND THE TEXT

1. People travel in different ways to get from one place to another. How have you travelled to different places?
2. What type of travel have you not tried yet? What type of travel would you like to try?
3. Riding on horses or in wagons takes longer than driving a car or flying in a plane. What are some other disadvantages of riding on a horse or in a wagon? What are the benefits of riding on a horse or in a wagon?
4. In the future, do you think people will be able to travel to space on holiday? What might that be like?

TIME TO WRITE

Write about your favourite way to travel. Explain why it is your favourite.